CHEERLEADING

CHEER TRYOUTS AND TRAINING

By Anita Banks

SportsZone
An Imprint of Abdo Publishing
abdobooks.com

abdobooks.com

Published by Abdo Publishing, a division of ABDO, PO Box 398166, Minneapolis, Minnesota 55439.

Printed in the United States of America, North Mankato, Minnesota
052024
092024

Cover Photo: Justin Ford/Getty Images Sport/Getty Images
Interior Photos: Matt Patterson/AP Images, 4–5, 29; Bryan Cerijo/Miami Herald/AP Images, 6; John Durán/GDAPhoto/AP Images, 8–9; Natalie Kolb/MediaNews Group/Reading Eagle/Getty Images, 11; Chatchai Somwat/Alamy Live News/Alamy, 12; Ken Murray/Icon Sportswire/AP Images, 14–15; Frank Mattia/Icon Sportswire/Getty Images, 16; Michele Eve Sandberg/Corbis/Icon Sportswire/Getty Images, 19; David Buono/Icon Sportswire/Getty Images, 20–21; iStockphoto, 23; Lynne Sladky/AP Images, 24; Matthew Lynch/Cal Sport Media/ZUMA Press/AP Images, 26–27

Editor: Christa Kelly
Series Designer: Kate Liestman

Library of Congress Control Number: 2023949391

Library of Congress Cataloging-in-Publication Data

Names: Banks, Anita, author.
Title: Cheer tryouts and training / by Anita Banks
Description: Minneapolis, Minnesota: Abdo Publishing, 2025 | Series: Cheerleading | Includes online resources and index.
Identifiers: ISBN 9781098293512 (lib. bdg.) | ISBN 9798384912781 (ebook)
Subjects: LCSH: Cheerleading--Juvenile literature. | Tryouts--Juvenile literature. | Skills training--Juvenile literature. | Sports--Juvenile literature.
Classification: DDC 791.6--dc23

TABLE OF CONTENTS

CHAPTER 1

BECOMING A CHEERLEADER

There are many types of cheerleaders. Some are school spirit leaders, encouraging fellow students at pep rallies and sporting events. Some participate in exciting competitions against other cheerleading teams. Other cheerleaders work professionally, entertaining crowds at big games.

No matter who they cheer for, all cheerleaders must work hard to be on a cheerleading team. The first step toward

Cheerleading is one of the most popular athletic activities in the United States.

LSU

making a team is typically tryouts. Tryouts are a series of tests that assess which candidates would be the best fits for a team. Aspiring cheerleaders usually perform in front of a coach or a judge.

Most professional cheerleaders must audition every year.

Tryouts can be stressful, but they can be fun, too. Being prepared for tryouts can make the experience less overwhelming and more exciting.

Once cheerleaders have made a team, they must work hard to learn the moves and cheers that make up the squad's routines. Most cheerleaders work out and attend practices multiple times each week. Cheerleading takes a lot of commitment, but with enough hard work, anyone can excel at the activity.

THE HISTORY OF CHEERLEADING

Cheerleading is more than 100 years old. The first cheerleaders were known as yell leaders. They led cheers at college football games. Today, there are almost 3.5 million cheerleaders in the United States and millions more worldwide.

CHAPTER 2

FINDING A CHEER SQUAD

When joining a cheer team, prospective cheerleaders should first decide what type of cheerleading they're interested in. There are several different options. Age and skill level can help determine which team an athlete should choose.

YOUTH RECREATIONAL CHEER TEAMS

Beginning cheerleaders can start on a youth recreational team. Also known as

Some youth recreational cheer teams attend competitions.

BEARS
CAMPEONES
Primer Lugar
VISITADO
TIME OUT
SUBCAMPEONES
Bears

rec or club teams, these groups are great places for new cheerleaders to learn basic skills. These clubs often perform at community sporting events, which can help new cheerleaders get used to performing in front of crowds.

Rec cheer teams are mostly made up of athletes in elementary and middle school. Most of the members are learning cheerleading skills for the first time. Youth cheerleading clubs normally accept all applicants, regardless of skill or experience.

SCHOOL CHEER SQUADS

Cheerleaders who want to support their school can join their school cheer team. Many middle schools, high schools, and colleges have cheerleading squads. Some teams hold tryouts, while others let anyone participate.

High school squads are often divided into junior varsity and varsity teams. Junior varsity teams are typically made up of younger or less experienced cheerleaders. Varsity teams consist of older or more experienced cheerleaders. Both teams perform at pep rallies and school sporting events. During games, they use cheers, tumbling skills, and stunts to motivate players and keep crowds excited.

Cheerleaders contribute to their communities in many ways, including participating in parades.

There are more than 150,000 All Star cheerleaders.

These teams also occasionally compete in cheer competitions.

ALL STAR CHEERLEADERS

All Star cheerleading teams compete against other teams at local, regional, and national competitions. These teams perform complex routines that are carefully choreographed. Trained judges award teams points for advanced skills, synchronized moves, and showmanship. Each team tries to earn as many points as possible. Whichever team earns the most points with their performance wins.

All Star cheerleading programs are divided into seven levels of difficulty. Level seven is the most difficult. These cheerleaders can perform the most challenging skills. Programs host tryouts for cheerleaders to determine the best team in which to place each cheerleader. Reaching the higher All Star cheerleading team levels can be competitive. The members of these teams are usually very experienced. Many have gymnastics and dance training.

CHAPTER 3

TRYOUTS

Most cheerleading teams hold tryouts. Tryouts help coaches determine each candidate's skill level so they can choose the best members for their team.

Tryouts are unique for each team. In order to feel prepared, it's important for new cheerleaders to learn as much about a team's tryout process as possible. Prospective cheerleaders can talk to coaches and current team members

Coaches look for cheerleaders who work well in a team.

Prospective cheerleaders should practice tumbling passes to perform for coaches at tryouts.

to learn what to expect at tryouts. Candidates should listen carefully and follow the advice the coaches and team members share.

GETTING READY

Prospective cheerleaders should start preparing for tryouts as early as possible. Staying fit is one way to prepare. Cheerleading tryouts can be exhausting. Candidates should get their bodies used to strenuous exercise. Running, biking, and swimming are all great ways to get in shape. Prospective cheerleaders should also be stretching every day to keep their bodies flexible.

Candidates can also include specific cheerleading skills in their workouts. Practicing jumps and tumbling skills can help them prepare for the big day. If a team shares specific skills it will be testing in tryouts, prospective cheerleaders can practice them.

Some teams host clinics to help prepare cheerleaders for tryouts. These sessions can be valuable resources. The clinics often teach candidates the skills they'll need for tryouts.

TRYOUTS

On the big day, cheerleaders should arrive at tryouts early. This will give them plenty of time to prepare. Cheerleaders should wear comfortable athletic clothes. They also need to remember to bring any required paperwork.

Depending on the team, tryouts might take a few hours or involve several sessions spread out over multiple days. During tryouts, prospective cheerleaders perform dances, cheers, tumbling skills, and short routines in front of judges. The judges are usually coaches and team captains. They evaluate how each candidate does. At the end of the tryouts, they'll choose their teams.

HANDLING DISAPPOINTMENT

Sometimes cheerleaders don't make the team, no matter how hard they practice. This can be frustrating and disappointing. Talking to a trusted friend or family member can help people work through these emotions. Cheerleaders should also remember to never give up. They should work on preparing for the next tryouts.

Candidates might feel nervous during tryouts. This is normal, but cheerleaders shouldn't let their emotions overwhelm them. Deep breathing can help them feel better. Even when they are nervous or make a mistake, candidates should try to smile, make eye contact with the judges, and have a positive attitude. Judges want cheerleaders who can perform well under pressure.

NFL teams hold cheerleading tryouts every spring.

CHAPTER 4

TRAINING WITH A TEAM

Once a team has been chosen, training can begin. Training is an essential part of improving as a cheerleader. During practices, coaches teach cheerleaders new skills and routines. Teams also learn to perform together as a group. Most teams practice two to four times each week. These practices each last about two hours. As cheerleaders practice, they grow stronger, more skilled, and more comfortable with their routines.

Cheerleaders have to perform in all kinds of weather, including rain.

Practices begin with warm-ups. These are easy exercises to get the cheerleaders' blood flowing to their muscles. This prepares them for exercise and helps prevent injuries. Stretches and jogs are common warm-ups.

Once cheerleaders are warmed up, they can move to more difficult exercises. Skill practice is an integral part of cheerleading training. Routines are made up of tumbling skills, stunts, dance moves, and jumps. Coaches teach cheerleaders to perform each of these skills safely.

STRETCHING

Some stretches are done while moving. These are called dynamic stretches. Arm circles, squats, and leg swings are all dynamic stretches. Static stretching is done while remaining still. Cross-body shoulder stretches and standing quad stretches are examples of static stretches.

Stretching before exercise can improve performance.

These skills are often introduced on mats or trampolines before cheerleaders attempt them on performance surfaces.

Cheer practice is another important part of cheerleading training. Cheers and chants motivate both fans and players. These shouts are often paired with synchronized movements. Cheerleaders may use props, such as pom-poms, to accentuate their movements.

Once cheerleaders are comfortable with their skills, they can begin practicing their routines.

Some choreographers, such as Natalie Chernow, have experience as both cheerleaders and cheerleading coaches.

These are often created several months before the first performance. They may be designed by coaches, cheerleaders, or even professional choreographers. Routines are often only a few minutes long but are packed with dozens of moves. Cheerleaders need to be synchronized for a routine to be safe and impressive. Some practices are almost entirely devoted to learning and perfecting a single routine.

Once practice is over, cheerleaders finish with a cooldown. Cooldowns are easy exercises designed to slowly lower an athlete's heart rate and blood pressure. These exercises help muscles recover from strenuous activity. Cooldown exercises can include stretches and short walks.

Cheerleading training is hard work, but it can be a lot of fun. It's exciting to learn new skills and cheers. Training also helps build relationships between team members.

CHAPTER 5

TRAINING ON YOUR OWN

Cheerleaders need to be in good physical shape. Staying in shape requires regular workouts. While training with a team provides regular exercise, some cheerleading teams practice for only part of the year. During the rest of the year, cheerleaders work out independently. The first step in this process is creating an exercise plan. These will look different for each

While consistent exercise is important, cheerleaders must also give their bodies time to rest.

BU
BU

athlete depending on their individual skills, goals, and fitness.

Training sessions should begin with warm-ups. After warming up, cheerleaders should do a cardio exercise. Cardio exercises help build endurance. Running, jumping rope, dancing, or biking are all good cardio options.

Athletes should do different exercises during each workout rather than doing the same form of exercise each day. Different exercises will condition different areas of the body. This helps with overall fitness. It can also reduce muscle overuse, which can prevent injuries. Workouts should end with a cooldown.

NUTRITION

Nutrition is a vital part of staying fit. To stay strong and healthy, cheerleaders need to fuel their bodies with proper nutrition. Protein, fruits, and vegetables are all parts of good nutrition. A protein-rich snack 30 to 90 minutes before practice gives the body the energy it needs for a workout. Protein-rich foods include eggs, dairy, nuts, meat, and beans. Doctors can help cheerleaders make sure they're getting the right nutrition.

Healthy bodies also need a lot of water. Cheerleaders need to hydrate their bodies before, during, and after exercise. Cheerleaders should always have a water bottle with them. They should try to drink at least 11 cups (2.6 L) of water each day to avoid dehydration.

Cheerleading is a fun and exciting activity. Participants get strong, learn new skills, and make new friends. Tryouts, practices, and workouts can be difficult, but seeing a stunning routine come together makes the hard work worth it.

Cheerleading is a great way to stay active and build confidence.

GLOSSARY

cardio
Exercises that increase a person's heart and breathing rates to make their heart and lungs stronger.

choreographed
Something that has been planned, often referring to a routine.

choreographer
Someone who creates routines for dancers or cheerleaders.

clinic
A class.

endurance
A person's ability to keep doing something.

evaluate
To determine how good something is.

nutrition
What a person eats and drinks.

pom-pom
A ball-shaped prop usually made of shiny pieces of plastic or foil.

prop
An object such as a pom-pom, flag, or megaphone that is used to enhance a cheerleader's routine.

recreational
Something done for fun rather than competitively or for a job.

routine
A performance made up of individual stunts, tumbling moves, jumps, and dance moves.

squad
A cheerleading team.

stunt
A skill in which a cheerleader is supported above the ground by one or more teammates.

synchronized
Performed at the same time as another person.

tumbling
Gymnastics skills such as cartwheels and flips.

MORE INFORMATION

BOOKS

Moffatt, Ali, and Alana Potter. *The Cheerleading Book: The Young Athlete's Guide*. Firefly, 2020.

Mooney, Carla. *Competitive Cheerleading*. Abdo, 2025.

Troupe, Thomas Kingsley. *Cheerleading*. Crabtree, 2022.

ONLINE RESOURCES

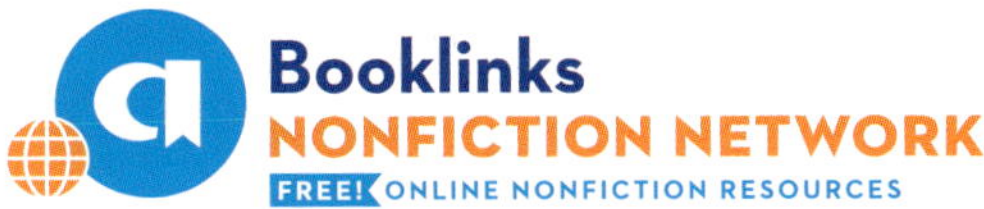

To learn more about cheer tryouts and training, please visit abdobooklinks.com or scan this QR code. These links are routinely monitored and updated to provide the most current information available.

INDEX

ABOUT THE AUTHOR

Anita Banks enjoys writing for children. She also enjoys reading, hiking, and traveling. Once upon a time, she was a cheerleader.